Dear Parent:

Congratulations! Your child is taking
the first steps on an exciting journey.
The destination? Independent reading!

STEP INTO READING® will help your child get there. The program offers
five steps to reading success. Each step includes fun stories and colorful art.
There are also Step into Reading Sticker Books, Step into Reading Math
Readers, Step into Reading Phonics Readers, Step into Reading Write-In
Readers, and Step into Reading Phonics Boxed Sets—a complete literacy
program with something for every child.

Learning to Read, Step by Step!

Ready to Read   Preschool–Kindergarten
• big type and easy words • rhyme and rhythm • picture clues
For children who know the alphabet and are eager to
begin reading.

Reading with Help   Preschool–Grade 1
• basic vocabulary • short sentences • simple stories
For children who recognize familiar words and sound out
new words with help.

Reading on Your Own   Grades 1–3
• engaging characters • easy-to-follow plots • popular topics
For children who are ready to read on their own.

Reading Paragraphs   Grades 2–3
• challenging vocabulary • short paragraphs • exciting stories
For newly independent readers who read simple sentences
with confidence.

Ready for Chapters   Grades 2–4
• chapters • longer paragraphs • full-color art
For children who want to take the plunge into chapter books
but still like colorful pictures.

STEP INTO READING® is designed to give every child a successful
reading experience. The grade levels are only guides. Children can progress
through the steps at their own speed, developing confidence in their
reading, no matter what their grade.

Remember, a lifetime love of reading starts with a single step!

Visit us on the Web!
StepIntoReading.com
Seussville.com
pbskids.org/catinthehat
treehousetv.com

Educators and librarians, for a variety of teaching tools, visit us at RHTeachersLibrarians.com

Library of Congress Cataloging-in-Publication Data
Rabe, Tish.
Step this way / by Tish Rabe ; from a script by Graham Ralph ; illustrated by Tom Brannon. — First edition.
   pages cm. — (Step into reading. Step 2)
"Based in part on The Cat in the Hat Knows a Lot About That! TV series"—Copyright page.
ISBN 978-0-449-81435-2 (trade) — ISBN 978-0-375-97163-1 (lib. bdg.) —
ISBN 978-0-375-98154-8 (ebook)
1. Brannon, Tom, illustrator. II. Ralph, Graham. III. Cat in the hat knows a lot about that! (Television program). IV. Title.
PZ8.3.R1145St 2013 [E]—dc23 2012047693

Printed in the United States of America
10 9 8 7 6 5 4 3 2 1

Step This Way

by Tish Rabe

from a script by Graham Ralph

illustrated by Tom Brannon

Random House 🏠 New York

"These shoes are cool," said Nick.
"But as you can see,
they may fit your dad
but they're too big for me."

"When I wear my mom's shoes," said Sally, "I fall.
Her shoes are too big and my feet are too small."

"Shoe trouble?" the Cat said.
"Well, I have some news.
Not everyone's feet can
fit in the same shoes.

"Feet come in all sizes,

and soon you'll see that

some are flippy, some flappy,

and some feet are flat.

"Want to see some neat feet?
Well, today I'll take you
to a faraway place:
Bing-Bungle-Ba-Boo!
It's a wonderful place
full of friends you will meet.
And each of them has,
oh, such different feet!"

In minutes they landed
in Bing-Bungle-Ba-Boo,
right by a lake,
and the Cat called, "Yoo-hoo!"

"Hello there, Cat! Welcome
to my lake," said a duck.
"Emily!" cried the Cat.
"There you are! We're in luck!

"Meet Emily, one of
my friends," said the Cat.
"As you see, her two feet
are all flippy and flat."

"It's true," said the duck.
"My feet are long and wide.
Let's swim and I'll race you
to the other side."

The kids tried their best,
but soon Sally said,
"We've fallen behind.
Emily's way ahead!"

"She won," said the Cat,
"and we came in last.
Her feet push the water
so she can swim fast.

"Duck feet are perfect
for swimming, it's true.
With my Flipper-ma-zippers
we can swim fast, too."

They swam really fast
and crossed the finish line.
Then they heard a voice call,
"Do you have feet like mine?"

"Nick and Sally," the Cat said,

"I'd like you to meet

Mikey the Lemur,

who hangs by his feet."

"Our feet aren't like yours,"
said Nick. "Not at all.
If we hung by our feet,
I'm afraid we would fall."

"I have lemur feet,"
said the Cat, "just for you.
Now you can hang
the way Mikey can do."

Before the kids knew it,
they were up in a tree.
"I can hang like a lemur,"
said Nick. "Look at me!"

"Try this!" Mikey said.

"You will think that it's neat.

You can hang upside down

just by using your feet."

"Lemurs are great climbers,"
a voice said, "but see?
Nobody is better
at climbing than me!"

"Greg the Gecko!" the Cat said.

"We're glad to see you.

Geckos have feet

that can stick just like glue."

"Tiny hairs," said Greg,
"help my feet to grip.
　　These hairs let me hold on
　　so I do not slip."

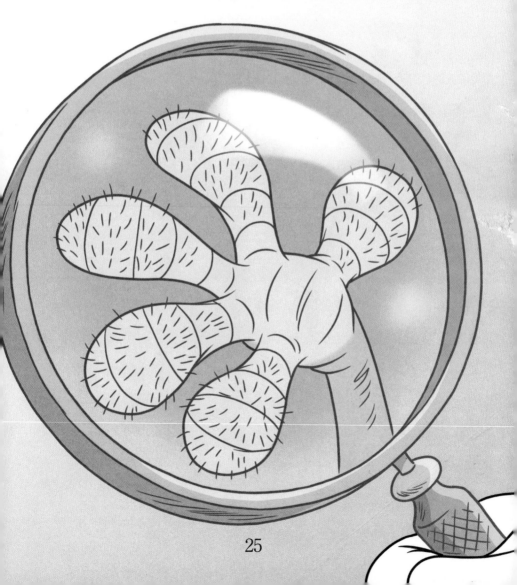

The Cat passed out gecko feet.

Nick said, "This is tricky.

I can't move at all.

My feet are too sticky."

"Look!" said the gecko.
"I'll show you my trick—
press and peel, peel and press,
and your feet will not stick."

They pressed and they peeled,
and the gecko was right.
They walked upside down,
and their feet held on tight.

"I can walk like a gecko!"
said Nick. "Who would guess
you can walk upside down
if you peel and you press?

"Try duck feet for swimming,
and lemurs' for gripping.
The feet of a gecko
will keep you from slipping.

"But, Sally, I think that
when we get back home,
I'll return your dad's shoes
and just wear . . .

"... my own!"